Medieval
Cats

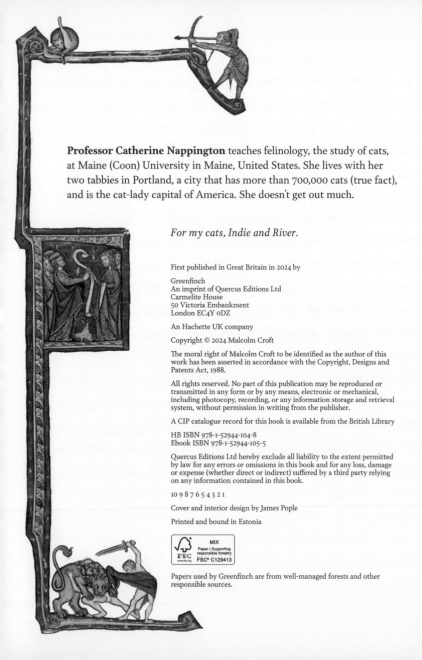

Professor Catherine Nappington teaches felinology, the study of cats, at Maine (Coon) University in Maine, United States. She lives with her two tabbies in Portland, a city that has more than 700,000 cats (true fact), and is the cat-lady capital of America. She doesn't get out much.

For my cats, Indie and River.

First published in Great Britain in 2024 by

Greenfinch
An imprint of Quercus Editions Ltd
Carmelite House
50 Victoria Embankment
London EC4Y 0DZ

An Hachette UK company

A CIP catalogue record for this book is available from the British Library

HB ISBN 978-1-52944-104-8
Ebook ISBN 978-1-52944-105-5

10 9 8 7 6 5 4 3 2 1

Cover and interior design by James Pople

Printed and bound in Estonia

MIX
Paper | Supporting
responsible forestry
FSC® C129413

Papers used by Greenfinch are from well-managed forests and other responsible sources.

Medieval Cats

Claws, paws and kitties of yore

Professor Catherine Nappington

greenfinch

dilx scalpens & effodient sibi ipsi conformat. Quidã ũ ex huĩ
natura impio seruire parata: terrã ab aliũ fossam. uentriq;
supmo imposita quatuor pedibx cõplectentes. lignoq; in ore
tñsuerso locato: demibx ab aliũ hinc inde coherentibx raw
gradeq; trahentibx: ũ absq; inuentum admiratione trahũt.

utio appellatus Musi
quod muribx in
festuũ sit. hunc
uulgus catum a captura
uocant. Alii dicunt qd
captat idest uidet. Hã
tam acutre cernit ut ful
gore luminis noctis te
nebras supet. Vnde a
greco uenit catus idz in
geniosus. apoтⷢⱶⱪₐ
ᵬₑₛₑⱥⱫ. Ous.

us pusillum animal grecũ illi
nomen est quicqd uero ex eo tra
hit: latinũ sit. Alii dicunt mu
res quod ex humore tre nascantur. Nam
mus tra. unde & humus. Tris implemlu
nio recur cresci. sicut quedã maritina
augentur: que rursus minuente luna deficiunt. Soꝛex latinũ
est eo qd rodat & in modum serre precidat. Antiqui aute
soꝛice sauricem dicebant. sicut & clodũ claudũ. Mistice aũ
mures significant hoĩes cupiditate terena inhⱬantes. & preda

A clowder of cats and a rat feeding on eggs, bestiary, *with
extracts from* Giraldus Cambrensis, *Harley 4751 f.30v, 13th
century. From the British Library archive/Bridgeman Images.*

YE OLDE CONTENTS

INTRODUCTION

he Middle Ages. What a fun time to be alive! It was an era of sieges and superstition, bloodshed and bloodlines, conquest and chaos. Between 500–1500 CE, mythical megastars such as Robin Hood and King Arthur rubbed muddy metaphorical shoulders with real-life legends such as Leonardo da Vinci and Joan of Arc, to name just two heroes of history. It was also a time before cutlery, underwear and flushable toilets and, boy, does it show. If the medieval ages were a modern Hollywood movie, critics would call it 'the bloodiest action-mystery-thriller-fantasy-horror-romance-drama ever made', with a 1,000-strong cast of lunatics, heretics, shamans, pagans, witches, warlords and dictators too unbelievable to lead the way – but most certainly did. It was a wild, wicked and weird time, no doubt. It comes as little surprise that nobody got out of it alive.

At the heart of all of this mayhem, there was a horse-and-cartload of curious medieval cats bearing witness – when they weren't napping in a nice warm spot, of course – to a rather epic thousand years of human misadventure. However, cats did more than just simply observe our shenanigans. They became integral to them (though not by choice). We squeezed them into our storytelling, our superstitions, our sin – even our language – almost as soon as the Dark Ages kicked in. At first, these domestic pets simply kept the rodents in check before being elevated to valued status symbols, creatures we allowed to pounce playfully across the parchment of important manuscripts, recorded with joy by their narrators. Alas, as the medieval age evolved across Europe, cats soon transmogrified into agents of evil in league with the devil, condemned to live their nine lives as mere puppets of sorcerors, according to the stupid and superstitious. (Cats work for no man, not even the Dark Lord; anyone who's ever met a cat knows that!) We can laugh about it now, but the end of the medieval era was not cool for cats. Thankfully, they landed on their paws and are now pretty much adored all over. As for humans, the jury's still out.

Anyway, welcome to this curious compendium that goes seriously medieval on cats. Inside, you'll find a catalogue of frisky felines from ye olde times of yester yore getting up to all sorts of fun – and a whole lot more. Now tell me, which medieval cat is *your* favourite?

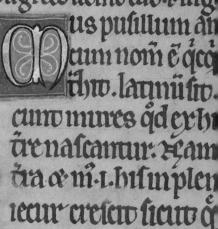

M[us]i[..]
lati[..]
mu[..]
infestis su[..]
uulgus ca[..]
captura u[..]
Alii dicun[..]
captat. i. u[..]
ream tam[..]
cernit. ut s[..]
luminis [..]

tenebras super. Vn á greco uento cab. i. ing[..]
us pusillum an[..]
cum non é q[..]c[..]
thro. latinu str[..]
cum mures q[..]d ex h[..]
tre nascantur: ream[..]
tra & m. i. his in plen[..]
recur crescit sicut q[..]

1.

THE CATT SATTETH UPON THE MATTETH

 edieval cats of all shapes and sizes strayed and sprayed the world for more than a millennium in the humble hope of finding a good home in which to nap on a nice warm lap. Because medieval cats loved nothing more than staying out of trouble, after all. Well, sort of...

Bestiary cats in illumination, St John's College MS 61, f.32v, c. 1200.
© *The President and Fellows of St John's College, Oxford.*

'I am a most faithful watchwoman, ever-vigilant in guarding the halls; in the dark nights I make my rounds of the shadowy corners — my eyes' light is not lost even in black caverns. Though I am a roving huntress and will pry open the dens of beasts, I refuse to pursue the fleeing herds with dogs, who, yapping at me, instigate cruel battles. I take my name from a race that is hateful to me.'

What am I?

'Riddle No.65', Aldhelm, Abbot of Malmsbury (a famed medieval riddler), Wiltshire, 700. The answer is 'mouser' – a medieval way of saying 'cat'.

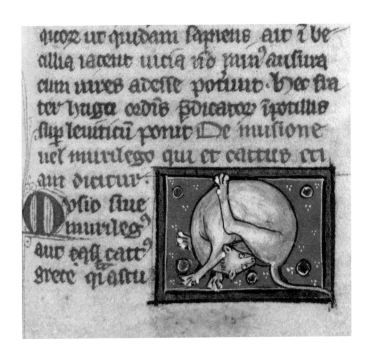

'Bum's out, tongue's out!'

Kitty lick, Bibliothèque municipale, MS 320,
f.73, Valenciennes, France, 1280.

'Didn't think this through, did I?'

Upside down cat, The Tudor Pattern Book, *Bodleian Library MS. Ashmole 1504, f.32v, 1464. © Bodleian Libraries, University of Oxford.*

'Cursed be the pesty cat that urinated over this book during the night.

And beware well not to leave open books at night where cats can come.'

One morning, in 1420, a Dutch monk found his beautiful manuscript ruined by cat wee. The monk was so annoyed he drew a picture of the cat and cursed it on the page – for all of eternity to see.

'Cock-a-doodle-dinner.'

'Unless need compels you, my dear sisters, you must not keep any animal – except a cat. Now, if someone needs to keep one, let her see to it that it does not annoy anyone or do any harm to anybody, and that her thoughts are not taken up with it.'

Ancrene Riwle, *Anonymous, 1225.*

The *Ancrene Riwle* was a code of conduct written by medieval monks for anchoresses, religious hermits, and the original crazy cat-ladies.

'I'd love a back scratch, thanks!
Oh, wait...'

*Close range cat attack, St John's College MS 61, f.12v, 1200. ©
The President and Fellows of St John's College, Oxford.*

'What do you call a book full of kitties? A catalogue!'

*Book lovers, Bibliothèque municipale, MS 0016,
f. 023v, Abbeville, France, 1475-1499.*

Pangur Bán

The most famous feline love letter that survives from the medieval period is the poem by Sedulius Scottus, an Irish monk in exile, writing about his white spotted cat, Pangur Bán, c. 900. In the poem, Scottus playfully compares his daily chores to that of his mouser.

I and Pangur Bán my cat,
'Tis a like task we are at:
Hunting mice is his delight,
Hunting words I sit all night.

So in peace our task we ply,
Pangur Bán, my cat, and I;
In our arts we find our bliss,
I have mine and he has his.

All domesticated cats descend from one genetic ancestor, *felis silvestris lybica*, from one common location: Africa.

'I am your king. Bring food.'

If looks could kill, Nicolaus de Lyra super Bibliam, *Italy, Latin MS 162, f. 252v, 1402. Image provided by The John Rylands Research Institute and Library, The University of Manchester.*

ebus uo n hñt n sp iste
ebit ipressu. Da g cp ps
ib ut pz ituen. ip cp die ra
destruy teplum vz. iplin
tuauit sic fecit ps onabud
lu testiu t ipr captiuauit
ie teplu t redificabz t uu
o eggabus t. b e sz ieio
ps iste pt eupi de afflictec
10 mlti in dei fuit t ffi er
antachi illustuo ip e tyra
fuger ad motes t ad alia
citatibz t uuil. ut hi i. mach
titate fuit subleuati pr
te recupauit t isideles de
des do inspu feit lr ps q di
gtoz t spa antachi mali
elo p spu z. debita pe c No
u mia r. qo dabit. Cep
us n e w cp culti dei uer

ossa collisa t tuo misablr mo
fusi st qm to sput coz i tu e f
ado i misso. cp ei fotue exat g
max i fusio s t toti creatu
libato euoi mia ilo do p mo o
num lr lbatois o. qo dabit eu
mishatibz inteplo cp erat i mi
remeduiz t antiachi t ei exat
qn do dedit ostatia t audatia i
pugno p ip q mathatias fui
cp fuit uer ut hi p mach zo
sue iducti p antachu exltab
fuit qn iudas machabe iplo
miate mudauer teplu t redi
rentes t gnudio mag ut hi
fm i leti ip mag ualet. O
gtoze i mal suis obstinato q lz
ti frio sr p apli ad tytu p cosu
uegur t mali do exainar t pu
cipit th snie de fa osidatio pi

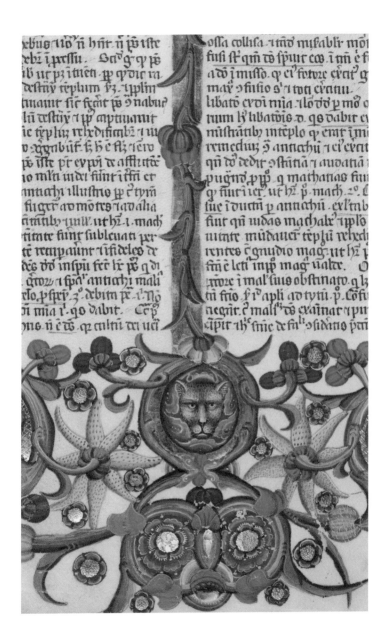

'Be quiet as a mouse... then POUNCE!'

A cat prepares to leap, MS 190, f.72r,
Cambrai Bibliothéque municipale, France, 1266.

'Let's take a cat, and feed him well with milk
And tender flesh, and make his couch of silk,
And let him see a mouse go by the wall,
Then he waives milk and flesh and all,
And every dainty that is in that house,
Such an appetite he has to eat a mouse.'

The Manciple's Tale, The Canterbury Tales, *Geoffrey
Chaucer, on cats as mousers, c.1400.*

The tradition of black cats symbolising bad luck began
in the medieval era. One particularly silly strand of
superstition stated that if a black cat walks towards you,
it is good luck...but if it walks away from you, it takes
the good luck with it – and leaves you with none!

'The cat is called musio, mouse-catcher, because it is the enemy of mice. Others say it gets the name from *capto* because it catches mice with its sharp eyes. For it has such piercing sight that it overcomes the dark of night with the gleam of light from its eyes. As a result, the Greek word *catus* means sharp, or cunning.'

Origin of the word 'cat', Aberdeen Bestiary, *1200.*

'Sorry, Jesus, but my bum's not gonna clean itself!'

Christ in Majesty (while a cat licks its bum), MA 112, f.7r, Germany, 1440-1460. From the New York Public Library.

'Wow! This stuff is *strong*.'

Cat super high on catnip, De natura animalium, MS 711,
f.23r, Bibliothèque municipale, Cambrai, France, 1270.

I wept and I wayled
The tearys downe hayled;
But nothinge it avayled
To call Phylyp agayne,
Whom Gyb our cat hath slayne.

The Book of Philip Sparrow, *John Skelton, 1525.*

John Skelton's famous poem about a young woman attending mass at a church in Norwich, England. Instead of prayer, however, she's thinking only about the brutal death of her pet sparrow, Philip, killed by Gyb, her cat.

'They mutter with their teeth closed and they feel in the dark towards where they saw their Lord and, when they find it, they kiss it, the more humbly depending on their folly, some on the paws, some under the tail, some on the genitals.'

De Nugis Curialium, *I.30, Walter Map, Archdeacon of Oxford, 1180.*

Medieval writer Walter Map on osculum obscenum (kissing a cat's anus), a ritual for worshippers of the devil, who would disguise himself on Earth as a black cat.

'I'm not fat! I'm cuddly!'

Fat cat, detail from a bestiary, England, MS 379, f.12r, 14th century. © Fitzwilliam Museum/Bridgeman Images.

'Did you hear about the cat who swallowed a ball of wool? She had mittens!'

Cat on drums, from a marginal cycle of images of the funeral of Renard the Fox, Book of Hours, MS W.102, fol. 78v 1, 1300. *From The Walters Art Museum, Baltimore.*

'Thou shalt not suffer a cat to live.'

Pope Gregory IX

On 13 June 1233, Pope Gregory IX, head of the Catholic Church, declared all cats, particularly black ones, demonic.

The widespread massacre of cats that followed in Europe helped spread the Black Death, a pandemic that killed more than 200 million people.

2.

KING CATTUS

or the first part of the medieval era, in the Dark Ages, cats were kings. They ruled the lands they roamed and partied with monks, priests and the ruling elite. Even kings and queens bowed down to cats to give them a cuddle. That's power you just can't buy.

All hail the one true king – King Cattus!

'A cat may look at a king'

A cat proverb from the 1500s meaning that even the lowest creature still has rights.

The Cat King, Scheibler'sches Wappenbuch, *BSB Cod.icon.312, p263 (left)* and *p49 (right), 1450. © Bayerische Staatsbibliothek, München.*

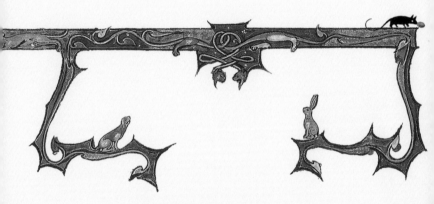

King Solomon's Cat

This popular medieval fable told tall tales of the last king of Israel, King Solomon, and his wise cat, a kitty so magical that it would hold a candle at a dinner table while the king dined.

The tale of *King Solomon's Cat* was first recorded in 1450 by Hans Vintler.

'All together now...
"Cat and the candle and
the silver spoon..."'

King Solomon's Cat, Die Plümen der Tugent, *Hans Vintler, cod.
s.n. 12819, f.130r, Wien Österreichische Nationalbibliothek, 1450.*

'Look what the cat dragged in – ME!'

Mad moggy, Buch der Natur, Konrad von Megenberg, MS.2.264, f.85r, 1434. Bibliothèque nationale et universitaire de Strasbourg, France.

Ireland's Witch

In 1324, Alice Kyteler became the first person condemned for witchcraft in Ireland. She is said to have summoned a demon that took the form of a black cat to help her poison all four of her husbands.

Kyteler escaped during her trial so her servant, Petronilla de Meath, was burned to death at the stake in her place, November 3, 1324.

'This is harder than it looks!'

Tybert, King of Cats

In medieval France, pet cats were called Tybert – the origin of the English pet name 'Tiddles'. The name Tybert rose in popularity due to the French folklore tales of Reynard, the trickster fox, who would often play pranks on his feline companion, Tybert.

The earliest mention of Tybert as the 'King of Cats' dates back to 1481.

Cat Fact #1

Other common pet names for medieval cats that have survived in manuscripts include Mite, Belaud, Meone ('little meow'), Cruibne ('little paws") and Breone ('little flame', no doubt for ginger cats).

'May the Dark Lord make us able, to eat all the mice on the table. Amen!'

Cat dinner party, MS. Laud Misc. 302, f.210r, mid-15th century. © Bodleian Libraries, University of Oxford.

'I'm going to Hell for this.'

A cat cosplaying as a nun, Book of Hours, Horae beatae
Virginia Mariae ad usum Romanum, cum calendario, *096
R66HF, folio 99r, State Library Victoria, Australia, 1490.*

Medieval Cat Proverbs #1*

In a cat's eye, all things belong to cats.

A cornered cat becomes as fierce as a lion.

A cat has nine lives. For three he plays, for three he strays, and for the last three he stays.

Curiosity killed the cat, satisfaction brought it back.

*The Middle Ages practically invented the cat proverb.

Kattenstoet

The origins of Kattenstoet, or 'The Cat Parade',
a Belgian festival devoted to the cat, are very
macabre. For centuries, every year on the second
Sunday of May, a dozen cats were thrown from
the tall belfry tower of Ypres's Cloth Hall to purge
the town of evil spirits contained within cats.
The last cat to take flight was back in 1817.

'Half cat, half goat, half asleep.'

'Call me Sir Claws-alot.'

Cheshire grin on a grey leopard, MS 320, f.67, Bibliothèque Municipale, Valenciennes, France, 1280.

'The catnip's kicking in...
I've got The Fear.'

Wild eyes, The Hague MMW, 10 B 25 f. 24v and 65v, 1450. From the Koninklijke Bibliotheek National Library of the Netherlands.

'Stroke me and you die.'

Top cat, The Hague MMW, 10 B 25 f. 24v and 65v, 1450. From the Koninklijke Bibliotheek National Library of the Netherlands.

In 945, Welsh King, Hywel Dda (above), valued cats so much he established laws that set out the duties of the cat and its monetary worth:

'The value of a cat, fourpence. The value of a kitten from the night it is born until it opens its eyes, a legal penny; and from then until it kills mice, two legal pence; and after it kills mice, four legal pence.'

'You're not riding me.
I'm carrying you. Got it?'

Cat carrier, Speculum historiale, *Vincent of Beauvais*, MS. 1301, f.
233r, *Bibliothèque Municipale, Boulogne-sur-Mer, France, 1294-1297.*

Diſimiliuz inſi on ſocietaſ.

'Nice to eat you, mouse!'

Cat who got the cream, Melchiorre Sessa, *University of Pennsylvania Libraries, Philadelphia, United States, C5 Al116 5320, 1506, 1533 and 1543.*

Raining Cats and Dogs

Some believe this famous medieval phrase has its origins from when ye olde English rain storms were so big they would float the bodies of dead animals in the streets (of which there were a lot) and wash them downstream.

'Hark, how she storms!
She is like to drown me in a shower of cats and dogs.'

Petruchio, Taming of the Shrew, William Shakespeare, Act 2, Scene 1, 1623.

3.

GET THEE TO A CATTERY

ats were beloved by most servants of God – when they weren't being tortured by fundamentalists or burned alive by superstitious Satanists, that is. It was the monks, after all, who studiously captured the spirit of cats on the pages of their illuminated manuscripts, the comprehensive records of these strange times...

Jacob claims his brother's birthright while the cat snacks on a rat, Book of Prayers, *MS Add. 20729, f.105v, Netherlands, c.1500. From the British Library archive/Bridgeman Images.*

William Shakespeare: Cat Lover #1

The world's greatest writer mentioned cats more than 40 times in his plays. They were rarely positive.

◇◇◇

'I am as vigilant as a cat to steal cream.'
Falstaff, Henry IV, Part I, Act 4, Scene 2, 1597.

'Good king of cats, I want to take one of your nine lives.'
Mercutio to Tybalt, Romeo and Juliet, Act 3, Scene 1, 1595.

'What though care killed a cat, thou hast
mettle enough in thee to kill care.'
Claudio, Much Ado About Nothing, Act 5, Scene 1, 1598.

'I could endure anything but a cat. And now he's a cat to
me... A pox upon him! For he is more and more a cat.'
Bertram, All's Well That Ends Well, Act 4, Scene 3, 1603.

atcↄ ſtercuſ   & ſinapem equiſ ponderibↄ ex aceto
concucu captuſ allopiciaſ ſanat·   Dptluuiu ex
partu. Catↄ ſtercuſ cu reſina & roſa   ſub poſitu
reprimit·   1 qu1s spiɴa 6 lutterit·⁊ ſpiɴa
catte ſtercuſ illintu. faucibↄ ·   ſine difficultate gↄ hit
           D QVARTAɴaS. Catↄ ſtercu cu ungula bouina
incollo uel brachio ſuſpenſu · quartaɴa poſt ſeptima ac
ceſſione diſcutit. ſed uide ne feſtineſ illudſoluere·

           D GRILLE aD Qv1 paraliſ1   teaptaɴtur
grilliſ ad epſ remediu afferet· hiſ qui paraliſi iteptant.
           D claritatem oculorum·
grilliſ & ſoriciſ combuſtioneſ cor melle miſcant & inde

'One lick, two lick, three lick, PAW!'

Cat licks its paw, Herbarium. Ex herbis femininis Liber
medicinae ex animalibus, *MS. Bodl. 130, f.90v, 1090.*
© *Bodleian Libraries, University of Oxford.*

len repaima a la gciu la gram
pleine de loi a nemis auoient
occis. Er li remanans sen estoit
fuis. li romain teuurent a
gram ioic a loi tentes. Coumt
[ ]esar en
tra en la
terie de
sens ꝯ
[ ]sar tn
puis v
me gnr

'Cats are a mysterious kind of folk. There is more passing in their minds than we are aware of. It comes no doubt from their being so familiar with warlocks and witches.'

Sir Walter Scott, Scottish poet and historian, c.1800.

'Jump... and I'll give you paws for thought!'

Cat teasing dog, Book of Hours (Thérouanne), Chronique de Baudouin d'Avesnes, MS. 1043 (863) f.69r, Médiathèque de l'Abbaye Saint-Vaast, Arras, France, 13th century.

'Cats are not impure, they keep watch about us.'

Muhammad, the medieval prophet of Allah (570–632) and founder of Islam, was famously a fan of cats. It is believed that he had a favourite cat, Muezza, whom he loved so much he would rather be without his garments than disturb the cat when it was sleeping upon them.

'Don't mind me. Just looking for a warm spot.'

'How can I trust you? You're a snake in the grass!'

Cat protects a sleeping baby, Sinbadnama: The Story of Sinbad, *I.O. ISLAMIC 3214, f.64v, c.1575. From the British Library archive/Bridgeman Images.*

hat vch vor deu katczen · vp vor ulecken vnde hinden kratzen

'Woah! These mice were spiked!'

Cat regrets its catch, woodcut, c.1500, unknown artist, Cooper Hewitt Smithsonian Design Museum, Wikimedia.

*Hüte dich vor den Katzen,
die vorne lecken und
hinten kratzen.**

('Beware of the cats that lick the front and scratch the back.')

**This German proverb has been attributed to the Protestant
reformer, Martin Luther, during the late Middle Ages.*

Transmogrification

The black cat was the perfect vessel for Satan to be a devil-in-disguise. When he did, he would take the name Grimalkin – the devil-cat.

'This kitten of ours is a cheeky little monkey!'

Monkey business, Trivulzio Book of Hours, *Royal Flanders, France, 1470. From the Library of Congress, World Digital Library.*

Ou chat na rat regne.

('Where there is no cat the rat is king.')

The origin of the famed proverb 'When the cat is away, the mice will play', is taken from the French iteration above, and first appeared in England in the 1470s.

'Scratch – and sniff!'

Butt attack, Rothschild Canticles, *Beinecke MS 404, 107v, 130r, 156v, 181r, 1300. Beinecke Rare Book & Manuscript Library, Yale University.*

'A cat is worth three cows if it is able to purr and keep its owner's house, grain store and kiln free of mice, but only half that it if is just good at purring.'

The Book of Kells, Dublin, Ireland, c.800.

∞∞∞∞∞∞∞∞∞∞∞∞∞∞∞∞∞∞∞∞∞∞∞∞∞∞∞∞∞∞∞∞∞∞∞∞∞∞∞

Ireland's most-famous illuminated medieval manuscript, *The Book of Kells,* has a whole section on kitties called the *Catslechtae*. It outlines the medieval code of conduct for owning a cat.

'I haven't slept in at least
20 minutes. I'm off for a nap.'

Wide-eyed cat, from the Catslechtae, The Book of Kells,
MS58, 183v, 048r. 076v, c.800. From the Library of
Trinity College Dublin, the University of Dublin.

'I'm all curled up with nowhere to go.'

A big ball of beautiful fur, Siyah Kalem School, 15th century. Pictures from History/Bridgeman Images.

Belling the Cat

The famous 12th century folklore fable, *Belling the Cat,* tells the tale of three wise mice who decide to tie a bell around a cat's neck so that they can hear it ahead of its attack. However, the mice cannot agree on which one of them should carry out the task and so the cat remains a threat. The moral of the story? Mice are stupid.

Paw Print

In 2013, while researching his PhD in the Dubrovnik State Archives, medieval scripture student Emir Filipović noticed several paw prints on the page of an Italian manuscript dated March 1445. Filipović's photos of the manuscript went viral on social media and remain hugely popular to this day.

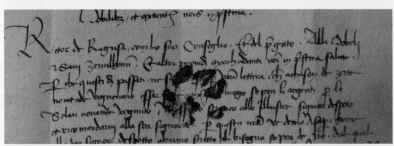

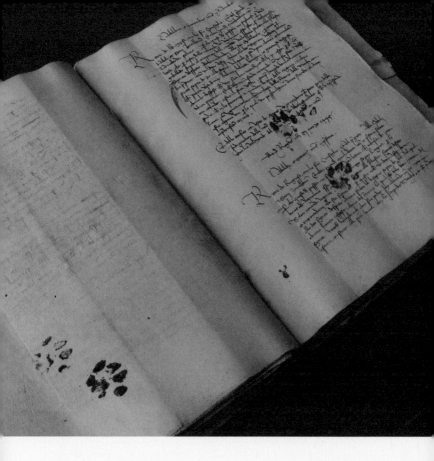

'It wasn't me – it was the dog!'

Inky paws, 'Lettere e commissioni di Levante', Italy, 1445.
© Emir Filipović/Dubrovnik State Archives.

Est bestia
que dicitur
eale mag-
nus ut equus cau-
da elephanti. in
gro colore. maxillis
aprinis. cornua
preferens ultra
modum longa ad
obsequium cuius uelit motus accommoda-
ta. Nec eorum enim rigent. sed mouentur ut
usus exigit preliandi. quorum alterum
cum pugnat pretendit. alterum replicat.
ut si ictu aliquo alterius acumen offende-
rit acies succedat alterius.

4.

MEOW & THEN

hroughout history, cats have endured an inconsistent relationship with people. In Ancient Egypt, cats were idolised by humans as gods. In the Middle Ages in Europe, cats were demonised by humans like devils. Cats have not forgotten either and so now they behave accordingly...

Creeping cat, bestiary, St John's College, MS 61, f.21r, 1200.
© The President and Fellows of St John's College, Oxford.

'Those who play with cats must expect to be scratched.'

Miguel de Cervantes, Spanish novelist, c. 1580.

'So, a cat, a priest and a monkey walk into a bar...'

Cat walks with a priest, Marco Polo, MS. Bodleian 264, f.96r, 1338. © Bodleian Libraries, University of Oxford.

il uit len plus entier nelune riens viuant
por cel fist alixand si com trouons lisant
se uuet que nus ientre qui lor aut forfaisat
Qui le tresor emport qui lauerra gisant
quat il sere mort ne uuet que nul se vant
Cesti a iiij. entrees mainent li paisant
De pierre ou de martel vont li auquat ferant
por escouter le son des harpes z le chant
Ni aura si hardi qui ost aler auant
Que se il i aloit de mort nauroit garant

fu haute la roche q la poit choisir
bien de iij lieues ne vous en quier mentir
Encore iporries autre merueille oir
Si poissies romture ne veoir ne sentir
Quant il ozent fait lueure trestout a lor plesir
Dun tout seul chapitel le font desus couurir
J. oisel de fin or por cel oeure acomplir
Font sus le chapitel par grant enging tenir
J. chalemel dargent li font du bec issir
Quel que vent que ientre quant il i puet ferir
Trestous autres oisiaus fait cele part venir
puis les font pardefors tout de fin or bruuir
Quant li solaus reluist tant le fait esclarcir

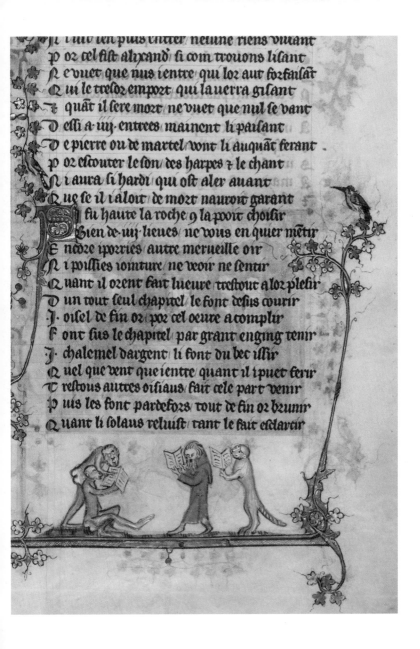

ceus misereatur nri et benedi
cat nobis illuminet uultum
suum super nos et misereatur nri
Et cognoscamus in terra uiam tuam
in omnibz gentibz salutare tuum
Onfiteantur tibi populi deus: con
fiteantur tibi populi omnes
etentur et exultent gentes qm iu
dicas populos in equitate: et gentes
in terra dirigis

'You sure look a lot like
my dinner tonight.'

Cat eyes its food, Book of Hours (Rome), *Cambridge MS B. 11.22, f.092v, 1300. From The Master and Fellows of Trinity College, Cambridge.*

'He is a right heavy beast in age and full sleepy, and lieth slyly in wait for mice: and when he taketh a mouse, he playeth therewith, and eateth him after the play. And he maketh a ruthful noise and ghastful, when one proffereth to fight with another: and unneth is hurt when he is thrown down off a high place.'

Bartholomaeus Anglicus, on cats, De proprietatibus rerum (On the Properties of Things), *1240.*

Bartholomaeus's *De proprietatibus rerum* was the first printed encyclopaedia and was widely cited in the Middle Ages. It is the most important compendium of medieval knowledge for scholars today.

Medieval Cat Proverbs #2

It takes a good many mice to kill a cat.

Cuirm lemm, lemlacht la cat.
(Beer with me, fresh milk with a cat.)
Irish

Make yourself a mouse and the cat will eat you.

Whenever a rat teases a cat, he is leaning against a hole.

A cat is a lion in a jungle of small bushes.

Aussi aise que ung chat qui ce baingne.
(As comfortable as a cat in a bath.)
French

'Eeny, meeny, miny...moe!'

A cat amongst the birds, De Venatione, *a Greek treatise on hunting, 11th Century.* © A. Dagli Orti/ © *NPL – DeA Picture Library/Bridgeman Images.*

'Scratch me if you can!'

*Monster cat, supposedly spotted on 18 February, 1568,
Leicester, drawing by the Commissary of the Ecclesiastical
Court for the Earl of Huntyngdon, Lansdowne MS 101/6, 1568.
From the British Library archive/Bridgeman Images.*

King Arthur's Quest

The giant devil cat of Arthurian legend, Cath Palug (the Clawing Cat, in Welsh) roamed the Isle of Anglesey, Wales, until King Arthur himself went on a quest to kill the horrible beast. In the battle, Cath Palug licked its claws when they were wet with Arthur's blood. The king was said to have lost an arm in the fight.

The tale was first recorded in the 1200s.

According to medieval superstition, to reverse the bad-luck curse of a black cat crossing your path, first walk in a circle, then walk backward across the spot the cat crossed and count to 13. Only then will the curse be lifted.

'Could you put some clothes on at least?'

'Quiet! I heard someone open a tin.'

Tabby cat, De animalium proprietate, *Manuel Philes, Burney MS 97, f.21, France, 1550. From the British Library archive/Bridgeman Images.*

Domine labia mea
aperies. **E**t os meum:

'When I play with my cat,
how do I know that she is
not passing time with me
rather than I with her?'

Michel de Montaigne, French philosopher, c. 1560.

'Hello darkness,
my old friend...'

Cat plays a lyre, Book of Hours, MS 662, f.21r, 15th century.
Beinecke Rare Book & Manuscript Library, Yale University.

'For the pain and blindness in the eye, take the head of a black cat, which hath not a spot of another colour in it, and burn it to powder in an earthen pot leaded or glazed within. Then take this powder and through a quill blow it thrice a day into thy eye. And so shall all pain flie away, and blindness depart although it hath oppressed thee a whole year: and this medicine is approved by many Physicians both elder and later.'

Edward Topsell, on his 'approved' potion to cure blindness,
The historie of foure-footed beastes, *1607.*

'Edward, you're an idiot.'

'Mouse, it's not my fault you taste so delicious.'

Cat takes a bite, De natura rerum, *Thomas de Cantimpre, MS Add. 11390 f.21, 13ᵗʰ century. From the British Library archive/Bridgeman Images.*

'Time to take a catnap – bonk!'

The devil attacks a cat from behind as another cat watches on, Expositio
in Apocalypsim, *Alexander Minorita, MS Mm.5.31 54v, 1249. Reproduced
by kind permission of the Syndics of Cambridge University Library.*

'If any beast has the devil's spirit in him without doubt it is the cat, both the wild and the tame.'

Edward, Duke of York, 1406.

'Who you calling a beast?'

In Ancient Egypt, cats represented a positive symbol of female sexuality, as seen through the depictions of Bastet, the black cat goddess.

Throughout prudish medieval Europe that positive symbol of female sexuality corroded. The word 'puss' arrived in the developing English language around 1533 and described anything that was 'soft, warm and furry'. It wouldn't be long before a derogatory term we all know (and loathe) came to describe a woman's genitalia...and weak men.

'Get your own damn penis!'

Nun trades fish for penis, (Flaisch macht Flaisch; flesh for flesh), woodcut, unknown artist, Netherlands, 1555. From the Rijksmuseum, Netherlands.

5.

GYBS & GRIMALKINS

ome cats of the medieval era were considered – falsely – to be Satanic spirits of the supernatural realm, more likely to lap up sorcery than a saucer full of cream. They were called grimalkins. Domesticated cats – known as gybs – got the better end of the broom and were loved by those who looked after them.

Cat plays a musical instrument, Book of Hours, Paris, MA 47, f.29r, 1450. From the New York Public Library.

'A kitten roves about following the straw; even if you are clever, you will scarcely induce an old cat to this trick.'

Egbert of Liége, The Well-Laden Ship (*Fecunda ratis*), *11th century.*

Egbert's Latin poem was full of ancient and medieval proverbs, fables and folktales. It also featured the earliest forms of nursery rhymes and fairytales, including 'Little Red Riding Hood'.

'Still trippin', man.'

'I'm armed...and dangerous.'

Two cats steal a rat while a guard dog snoozes, bestiary, MS. Bodleian 764, f.51r, 1226. © Bodleian Libraries, University of Oxford.

eternui
i.

milita
eam t
ne:qa
um ob
ca tridi
redme
uuum
ame.

Cat got your tongue?

Everyone's favourite English idiom, 'Cat got your tongue?', dates back to the Middle Ages, when superstitious people believed that a witch's black cat could steal, or paralyze, a person's tongue, leaving them unable to speak.

The phrase has origins in Ancient Egypt, when pharaohs were known to cut out a criminal's tongue as punishment...and feed it to their pet cat.

''Tis but a scratch!'

Cat and knight fight, Book of Hours, *MS Stowe 17, f.112, 1320. From the British Library archive/Bridgeman Images.*

'I will never buy the pig in the poke
There's many a foul pig in a fair cloak.'

Thomas Heywood, c.1550.

The phrase 'Let the cat out of the bag' dates back to
the mid-1500s and started life as 'a pig in a poke':
to buy something without first inspecting it.

At medieval markets, devious farmers would
often trick customers by selling them a cat in a
bag instead of a suckling pig. When the customer
returned home and opened the bag – or poke – the
cat sprang out of the bag and revealed the truth.

'Schrödinger, you crazy cat!'

Cat in a box, De herbis femininis, MS Sloane 1975, f.86v, France, 1275. From the British Library archive/Bridgeman Images.

'What's new, pussycat?
Woah woah woah woah!'

Cat looks surprised by its own musicality, Book of Hours, *Bruges,*
W.438, fol. 161v, 1480. From the Walters Art Museum, Baltimore.

96

William Shakespeare:
Cat Lover #2

'I am as melancholy as a gib cat or a lugged bear.'
Falstaff, Henry IV Part I, Act I, Scene 2, 1597.

'The cat, with eyne of burning coal,
Now couches fore the mouse's hole.'
Gower, Pericles, Prince of Tyre, Act 3, Scene 1, 1607.

'But will you woo this wild-cat?'
Katharine, Act 1, Scene 2, Taming of the Shrew, 1591.

'Playing the mouse in absence of the cat, to
tear and havoc more than she can eat.'
Westmoreland, Henry V, Act 1, Scene 2, 1596.

'Don't worry, even a dead cat
will bounce from a great height!'

A greedy cat killed by the owner of pigeons, The Lights of Canopus, *Persia,
MS W.599, fol.81b, 1264. From the Walters Art Museum, Baltimore.*

'When ye see a cat sitting in a window in the sun and she licks her bottom, and that one of her feet is above her ear, ye need not doubt that it shall rain that day.'

Jean d'Arras, on cat ailuromancy, The Gospelles of Dystaves, *1480.*

'To the shops, please!'

Ailuromancy
The practice of predicting the future, especially the weather, by observing a cat's movements.

This superstition is based in some biological truth. A cat's super-sensitive whiskers can detect a drop in low pressure, an indicator of stormy weather.

et religione vpiana au pectus. suo pma
tibi connenuit vtte qz ee noblis vieni
et margarita pulchima comprobaris. fz
timu tibi non conenit ut puella tam ple

'I can smell a rat.'

A curious magpie gets up close and personal, Legenda
Aurea, *Jacobus de Voragine, MS 808, f. 88v, Médiathèque
Toussaint, Bibliothèque municipale, France, 1367.*

Taghairm

In medieval Scotland, the ritual of Taghairm involved
a person roasting a cat alive above an open flame
and turning it on a spit. As the kitty caterwauled in
pain, the devil would appear. The Dark Lord would
then barter for the cat's life by offering the person
a glimpse into their future. Huge news, if true.

'Feel the pain of my paws, dog!'

A cat and dog fight, Book of Hours, *Paris, MS Add. 29433, f.20,
c.1407. From the British Library archive/Bridgeman Images.*

Cat Burning

This brutal religious ritual occured annually in Paris, France, where on the summer solstice, every 20 June, Parisians gathered in their thousands at the Place de la Grève, a traditional site for execution by guillotine, and watch as dozens of cats were hung above a flaming-hot pyre and roasted alive. Afterwards, the kings and queens threw a feast to celebrate the cleansing of evil, all while unaware of the irony.

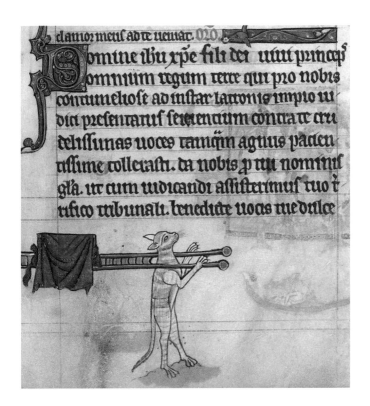

'Not sure we need the ladder. I always land on my paws.'

Tybert the Cat carries a ladder for Reynard the Fox, Book of Hours, Paris, W.102.77R, 1300. From the Walters Art Museum, Baltimore.

'Go get 'em, tiger!'

A cat attacks the mice which disturb the tiger, The Tutinama (Tales of a Parrot), *India, 1560. Gift of Mrs. A. Dean Perry/Bridgeman Images.*

Grimalkin, the foul Fiend's cat.
Grimalkin, the Witche's brat.

Medieval Rhyme

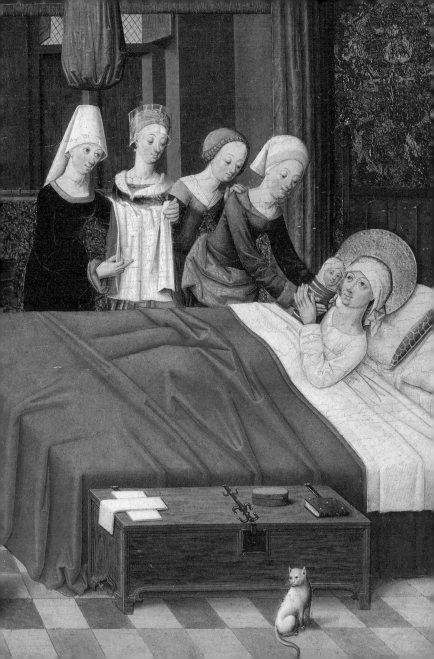

6.

BEWARE THE CATT

e honest – cats can sometimes deserve the trouble they find themselves in. No cat's *purr-fect*, after all. So don't let their cute little furry faces distract you from the truth: cats can be wicked little devils too...

Birth of the Virgin, 1485, panel from Stories from the Life of Mary, Master of the Aachen Altar, *Germany, 1485.* © A. Dagli Orti/© NPL – DeA Picture Library/Bridgeman Images.

Galeſia

lata alio noie
ta pes lepori
m. unda herba bene
garioſ. fillatim
fila ti ē quedā
cōfectio.

. Gatus ſiue gata q̄
latine muſipula . dr̄ .

Cat At A Cathedral

From 1305 to 1467, Exeter Cathedral, England, officially employed cats as ratters and mousers – and were on the payroll to prove it. The cathedral's accounts of the time showed payments of a penny a week *pro cato* (for the cat) to pay for additional food if the vermin it ate wasn't sufficient. A cat-hole in the cathedral still exists today and is considered the world's oldest surviving cat flap.

'Fancy a game of Hide and Squeak?'

Cat creeps up on a mouse, botanical illustration, MS Sloane 4016 f.40, Italy, c. 1440. From the British Library archive/Bridgeman Images.

Piloerection

The upright raising of hair along the
back of a cat as a response to fear.

'Hair of the dog?
Try hair of the cat!'

*Scaredy cat, Book of Hours, Paris, Bodleian Library MS. Douce
62, f.139r, c.1400. © Bodleian Libraries, University of Oxford.*

In medieval Europe, when cats were considered in league with witches – seems daft to say that out loud now – a common punishment was to tie the witch in a sack along with her cat and a heavy rock, and throw them into a river.

'As you can see, this black cat is clearly cursed!'

Cat climbs up a rope, The Hague, KB, 72 A 24, fol. 313v, 1410.
From the Koninklijke Bibliotheek National Library of the Netherlands.

'Giddy up, humans! Faster!'

Humans carry cats, MS. Douce 62, f.129r, 1309. ©
Bodleian Libraries, University of Oxford.

Six Cat Stats

1. Cats can jump six times their own length.

2. A cat's sense of smell is 14 times stronger than a human's.

3. Cats have more than twice the amount of neurons in their brain as dogs (they're twice as smart).

4. Cats have 24 more bones in their bodies than humans.

5. A pet cat shares 95.6 per cent of its genome with a tiger.

6. A modern cat's average lifespan is 14 years. Medieval cats had an average lifespan of much less, around eight years (if they were lucky.)

'I'm more of a dog person.'

Agnes Waterhouse, from Essex, was the first person executed – by hanging – for witchcraft in England in 1566.

Waterhouse made her innocence hard to be believed when she confessed to possessing a demonic spirit, a black cat called Satan. She blamed the cat for killing her husband after it told her to do it. Worst. Excuse. Ever.

'Argh! The tongue's got the cat!'

Big cat tongue, De natura avium, *MS. Ludwig XV 4 (83.MR.174), fol. 3, 1277. From The J. Paul Getty Museum.*

'Trip hazard or not,
I've found the warm spot.'

Cat warming itself before a fire, from Book of Hours (Rome) *Add MS 38126 f.1v, c.1480. From the British Library archive/Bridgeman Images.*

Witchcraft Act

In 1563, as superstitious suspicions of cats
ran amok across medieval Europe, English
Parliament passed the Witchcraft Act.

This law stated that witches who were convicted of
killing a person – more often than not, the husband
– were to be hanged, often without a fair trial.

*'That butt better be clean.
I've got to lick that fur later.'*

500,000

The estimated number of witches and pagans – 85 per cent of whom were women – condemned to die by hanging, drowning or burning up until 1650 in medieval Europe, as a result of receiving convictions for witchcraft.

'What do you mean I've got a face like a cat's arse?'

A clowder of cats, Littera textualis, a didactic miscellany, containing a bestiary, MS Kk.4.25, f.74v, 1230. Reproduced by kind permission of the Syndics of Cambridge University Library.

quas tergo laraufs emittit. quando canes
in sequentes patitur. quarum aculeis in
pbitate subsequentiu repellit.

Cuniculus genus agrestium animaliu
dictus quasi caniculi. eo quod canum
in stagine capiantur. Furo a furuo dicitur.
Unde & fur. Bestiola est que cuniculos de ca
uernis perturbat.

Melo dictus uel quod sit rotundissimo
membro uel quod fauos petat. & assi
due mella capiat. De pelliculis uero melo
num fiebat pus indumentum quoddam
ad operis exercitium aptu: quod meloten
dicebant. Postmodum de pelle caprina factu:
peram uocabant. Uestis est a collo pendens
& precincta usq ad lumbos. Melo qui &
alio nomine tarus dicitur. eo quod acerri
mum sit animal. huius axungia contra
guttam ualet.

Pusio siue murilegus appellatus quod muuib;
sit infestus. hunc uulgus cattum. a capi
tura uocant. Alii quia captat idest uidet.
Nam adeo acute cernit. ut noctis tenebras su
su supet. Unde & a greco uenit catus. idest
ingeniosus. apo toycata. hic cu stomacu
cibo pregrauari senserit. festucas carpit.
ac glutit. ut uel ita uomitu prouocet.

Mus pusillum animal grecum illi nome
est. Quicquid uero ex eo trahit latinu sit.
Alii dicunt mures quod ex humore terre nas
cantur. Nam mus terra. Unde & humus.
Hir in plenilunio iecur crescit sicut que
dam maritima augentur. que rursum
minuente luna deficiunt. Sorex latinu
est eo quod rodat. & in modum serre
precidat. Antiqui aute sorice sauricem dice
bant sicut clodum. claudum.

ut sciamus hunc a
mare. Et quo loco tu
locaris nos digneris
collocare: In hoc ení
tu bearis cū tu potes
nos beare. Ignis
rubū ingreditur. rubz
igne non leditur. nec solu
um offenditur. moyses
hunc aggreditur. heret
stupensqz redditur. sed
uox diuina subditur. rei
qz causa panditur. Tande

Caterwauling

The term used to describe the shrill, wailing sound a cat makes when it's in pain, lost, or pissed off at its owner for not being fed in a timely manner. From the Middle English term *caterwrawen*, 'to cry like a cat'.

'Someone's licked their bottom recently, haven't they?'

Man and cat kiss, Book of Hours, *Marginalia, Cambrai, France, Walters Manuscript W.88, fol. 40r, 1300. From the Walters Art Museum, Baltimore.*

Vibrissae

The scientific name for whiskers. Cats have 24 whiskers in total, 12 per cheek. Without them, cats can lose all sense of their surroundings.

'Ready, aim...FIRE!'

Cat pounces for a bird, Biblia Porta, *Lausanne, France, U 964, f. 357v, c.1275. From the Lausanne Bibliothèque cantonale et universitaire.*

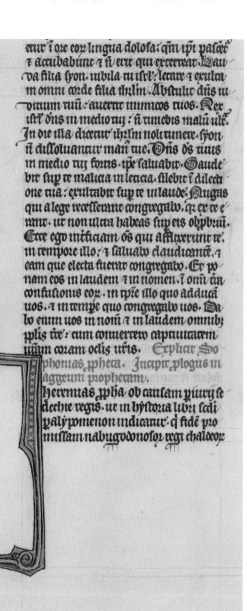

etur i ore eoz lingua dolosa: qm ipi pasceñ
z accubabunt z si erit qui exterreat. Lau
da filia syon. iubila tu isrl': letare z exulta
in omni corde filia ihrl'm. Abstulit dns iu
diciũ tuũ: auertit inimicos tuos. Rex
isrl' dns in medio tui: n timebis malũ ult.
In die illa dicetur ihrlm noli timere. syõ
ñ dissoluantur man tue. Dñs ds tuus
in medio tui fortis. ipe saluabit. Gaude
bit sup te malicia in leticia. silebit i dilecti
one sua: exultabit sup te in laude. Nugas
qui a lege recesserant congregabo. que ex te e
rant. ut non ultra habeas sup eis obpbriũ.
Ecce ego interficiam os qui afflixerunt te.
in tempore illo: z saluabo claudicantē. z
eam que electa fuerat congregabo. Et po
nam eos in laudem z in nomen. i omni ter
confusionis eoz. in tpe illo quo adducā
uos. z in tempe quo congregabo uos. Da
bo enim uos in noñ z in laudem omnibz
pplis tře: cum conuertero captiuitatem
uestram coram oclis uestris.   Explicit So
phonias ppheta. Incipit plogus in
aggeum prophetam.

Heremias ppha ob causam iurisiu
dechie regis. ut in hystoria libri sedi
paly pomenon indicatur: q fidē pro
missam nabugodonosor regi chaldeoz

rison du benoist gregon

7.

NIPPETH & NAPPETH

 ats can sleep with their eyes half open, a fact that pretty much tells you everything you need to know about this creature. Can it be trusted? Or is it just waiting for its chance to strike? For centuries, humans have assumed cats were just lazy, but really they're just biding their time...

Cat on a lap, scenes from the life of Saint Gregoire le Grand; Father of the Latin Church, Le Miroir Historial, Vincent de Beauvais, MS 722/1196 fol.10v, France, 1475. © Musée Condé, Chantilly/Bridgeman Images.

There is an estimated one billion cats worldwide. Approximately, 350 million of which are kept as pets, 500 million are stray or feral cats and 150 million are wild big cats. America has the most pet cats, with more than 75 million.

'You better not be aiming for a bullseye!'

Archer takes aim at a cat licking its bum, Biblia Porta, *Lausanne, France, U 964, f. 376r, c.1275. From the Lausanne Bibliothèque cantonale et universitaire.*

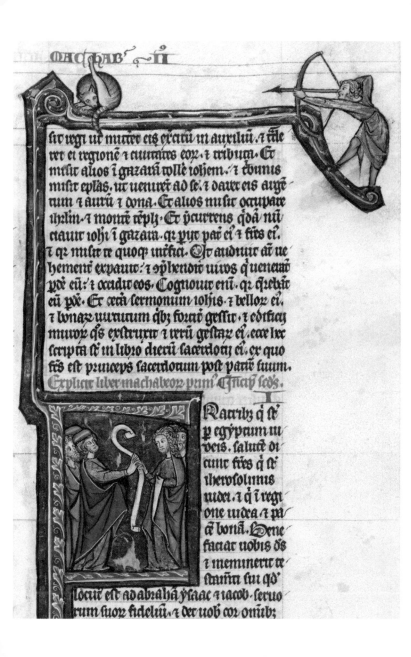

sit regi ut mittet eis exercitu in auxiliu̅. ⁊ tra-
det ei regione̅ ⁊ ciuitates eoℝ. ⁊ tributa. Et
misit alios i̅ gazaram tolle iohe̅. ⁊ thimis
misit ep̅las. ut uenir̅et ad se. ⁊ daret eis arge̅-
tum ⁊ auru̅ ⁊ dona. Et alios misit occupare
ihr̅l̅m̅. ⁊ monte̅ te̅pl̅i. Et p̅curre̅s q̅da̅ nu̅-
ciauit iohi̅ i̅ gazara. q̅ p̅yt pat̅ ei̅ ⁊ fr̅s ei̅.
⁊ q̅ misit te quoq̅ i̅t̅fici. Q̅s audiuit au̅ ue-
hem̅et̅ expauit. ⁊ o̅p̅hendit uiros q̅ uenerā̅t
p̅de eu̅. ⁊ occidit eos. Cognouit eni̅. q̅ q̅rebā̅t
eu̅ p̅de. Et cetᵃ sermonu̅ iohis. ⁊ belloℝ ei̅.
⁊ bonaℝ uirtutum q̅b̅z fortit̅ gessit. ⁊ edific̅z̅
muroℝ q̅s exstruxit ⁊ reℝ̅ gestaℝ ei̅. ecce hec
scripta st̅ i̅ libro dieℝ̅ sacerdot̅ij ei̅. ex quo
fc̅s est princeps sacerdotum post patre̅ suum.
Explicit liber machabeoℝ prim̅ Jncap sec̅s.

Patrib̅z q̅ st̅
p̅ egyptum i̅
deis. salute̅ di-
cu̅t fr̅es q̅ st̅
iherosolimis
iudea. ⁊ q̅ i̅ regi-
one iudea ⁊ pa-
ce̅ bona̅. Bene
faciat uobis d̅s
⁊ meminerit te
stame̅ti sui q̅d
locut̅ est ad abraha̅ ysaac ⁊ iacob seruo-
ru̅ suoℝ fideliu̅. ⁊ det uob̅ coℝ omnib̅z.

'A group of three cats is called a clowder, right? But surely a *claw-der* is better?'

A clowder of cats are helping (or hindering) a farmer, MS 16, 1475-1499, Bibliothèque municipale, Abbeville, France, 1475-1499.

Hypercarnivores

Cats are the only domesticated hypercarnivores in the whole world. Hypercarnivores are animals that require an absolute minimum of 70 per cent meat in their diet.

'Even humans look good enough to eat.'

Clowder

The collective noun for a group of cats. A group of more than three cats is also referred to as a clutter, a glaring or a pounce.

✕✕✕

A litter is the collective noun for more than three kittens, but the group can also be called a kindle or an intrigue.

'Come on, one bite won't hurt.'

A pet cat plays with a mouse, Luttrell Psalter, Sir Geoffrey Luttrell, Add 42130 f.190, c.1335. From the British Library archive/Bridgeman Images.

ies multitudini

runt ascendente

'Before I eat you, let me just
cough up this furball first.'

A cat looks down on its dinner, bestiary, England; MS Add. 11283,
f.15, c. 1170. From the British Library archive/Bridgeman Images.

Dewclaw

The name of a cat's fifth toe on its front paws. It allows cats climb to escape predators. Helpful for when a mob of pitchfork-waving maniacs want to throw you into a sack and beat you to death for being a demon.

'My favourite pet? A Trumpet!'

Cats are *digitigrades* – they walk on their toes, not their feet.

They also only move half of their body forward at once, walking with both right feet first, followed by both left feet. Females tend to put their right paws forward first and males tend to prefer their left. It's the reason cats look so elegant on their feet.

'A cat with a catapult is King!'

A cat in a tower aiming a catapult at mice, Book of
Hours, *England, Harley 6563 ff.71v-72, c. 1320. From
the British Library archive/Bridgeman Images.*

'Don't judge me. We all do it.'

*Cat cleans its bum as other cats look on, bestiary, MS. Douce
151, f.29v, 1300. © Bodleian Libraries, University of Oxford.*

Frappuccino

A cat's 'zoomies' were once considered a tell-tale
sign that it was possessed by the devil. Today we
know better. FRAPs, or Frenetic Random Activity
Periods, is the official term to describe the intense
but brief bursts of energy cats can get during the
evening. No one is quite sure why they do it – it
could be to wake themselves up before late-night
prowling or burning off energy after a catnap.

Isabeau of Bavaria

The 14th century queen of France, Isabeau of Bavaria, wife of Charles VI – the Mad King – loved her cat so much that in 1406 she spent an obscene amount of money – sixteen shillings! – on purchasing a tailor-made bright green cloth coat for it. Precisely the type of behaviour that led to the French Revolution.

'Monkey see, monkey do.'

The predator becomes the prey, The Harley Hours, England, MS Harley 92,8 f.44v-45, c.1275. From the British Library archive/Bridgeman Images.

'Pose for a portrait?
Don't you mean *paw-trait*?'

*Richard Whittington with his cat, line engraving by Renold
Elstrack, c. 1700. From Granger/Bridgeman Images.*

Dick Whittington & His Cat

The most famous medieval cat owner was Richard 'Dick' Whittington, London's Lord Mayor from 1397–1419. The legend of Dick Whittington tells the tale of a poor orphan boy who travelled to London to make his fortune with his rat-catching cat. Sadly, the real-life Whittington was neither poor, an orphan, nor owned a cat. Regardless, today a statue of a cat sits atop Whittington Stone at the foot of Highgate Hill, London.

'Time to give you some mouth-to-mouse resuscitation!'

Cat chases floor scraps, banquet scene, Ercole I d'Este Brevary, Biblioteca Estens, Modena, Italy. f.1, 1502. From © A. Dagli Orti/© NPL – DeA Picture Library/Bridgeman Images.

Ci commence le .vbiij. liure qui fait mencion
des proprietes des bestes.

ius que le traittie est acco
pli qui traitte de laorne
ment de la tir qut auv
choses qui issent de terre

8.

CURIOSITY KILLED THE CATT

he thousand-year-long medieval era showed humans that cats are the most curious of creatures. They love to stick their whiskers somewhere they're not wanted or find a new toy to play with. Sometimes that means paying the ultimate compensation...

Spot the cat, De proprietatibus rerum, *Bartholomeus Anglicus, MS 399, f.241, 1240. Bartholomaeus; Liber. From Bridgeman Images.*

'Mouse, consider me
a catastrophe!'

Mouser in action – sort of, bestiary, England, c.1250.
© Fitzwilliam Museum/Bridgeman Images.

Isaac Newton's Cat Problem

In 1687, while working on his gravity-defining experiments at Trinity College, Cambridge, Isaac Newton had to down tools as he was constantly getting interrupted by cats scratching at his door, wanting to come in. To stop the distraction, Newton asked a carpenter to cut two holes in his door – one for the mother cat and one for her kittens. It wasn't the first ever cat flap, but it did mean he could finish his work...and discover the laws of gravity.

Cats have the capacity to make more than 100 sounds, from distinct purrs to signature screeches and hisses, grumbly growls to melodic mewing and meowing. Dogs can only make 10 sounds. Idiots.

'The more you run, the more I have fun.'

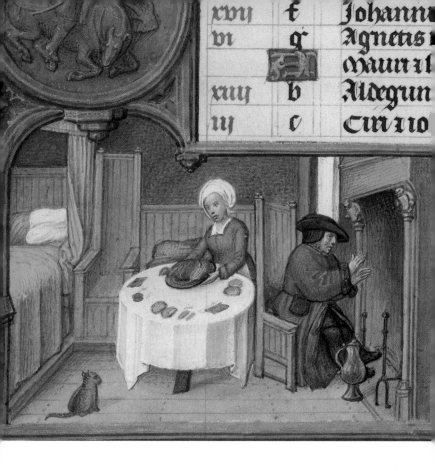

xvii   f   Johann
vi   g   Agnetis
      Maur il
xiiii   b   Aldegun
iii   c   Emerio

'Throw me a bone. I haven't eaten in minutes.'

Cat waits patiently for dinner scraps, Book of Hours, Bruges, c.1500, MS Add. 35313, f.1v. From the British Library archive/Bridgeman Images.

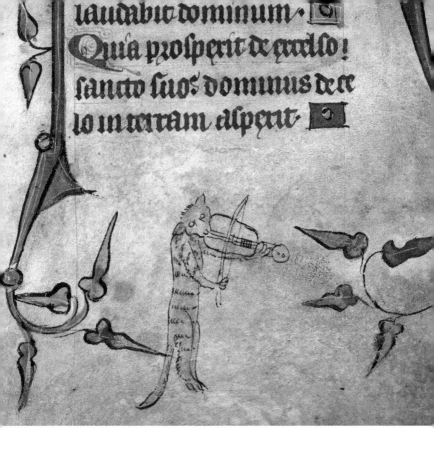

laudabit dominum ·
Quia prospexit de excelso ;
sancto suo: dominus de ce
lo in terram aspexit·

'It's better than my singing, trust me...'

Cat playing a rebec, a popular bowed string instrument from the medieval period, Book of Hours, England, Harley 6563, f.40, *c.1320. From the British Library archive/Bridgeman Images.*

Catgut Your Tongue

In the margins of many manuscripts, you'll find cats playing several stringed instruments. Scholars agree that this is a reference to catgut, natural fibres found in the walls of animal intestines, which were used for the strings of medieval musical instruments.

Cat Fact #2

One of the oldest inns in London, built circa 1500, was called Le Catt cum le Fydell (The Cat and the Fiddle). It was named after Caterine la Fidele, the first wife of King Henry VIII.

The Old English word 'catt', is believed to originate from the Latin word *cattus*, and first rose to popularity during the Dark Ages, around the sixth century.

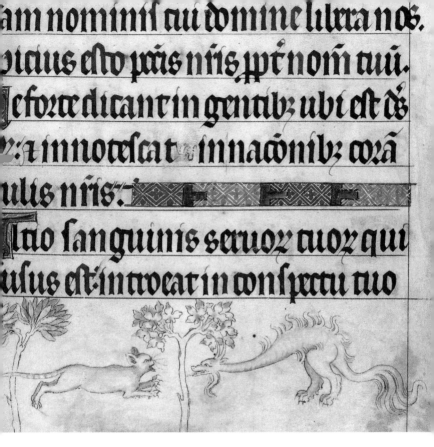

'Look what the cat dragooned in...'

Cat fights a dragon, The Queen Mary Psalter, *England, Royal 2 B. VII, f.188, 1310. From the British Library archive/Bridgeman Images.*

Domine exaudi o
ratione meam. & &
clamor meus ad te
ueniat. Oremus.
oncede Coff
nos famu
los tuos q̄
sumus domine deus
noster perpetua men
tis et corporis salute
gaudere: et gloriosa
beate marie semper
urginis intercessio

Piers Plowman

The first masterpiece of English literature from the period was the allegorical poem 'Piers Plowman' by William Langland, written in 1370 (ish). In it, Langland explores the obstacles faced by those trying to live a life of virtue in late-medieval England. He does this by using cats as a metaphor for the tyrannical powers of the ruling class spreading fear into the rats – the working class. As such, cats, Langland writes, should be killed 'for the sake of their skins'.

'My cat breath is stinky. I need a mousewash!'

Cat cleans its teeth with a mouse, Book of Hours (Maastricht), Netherlands, Stowe 17, f.129v, c.1325. From the British Library archive/ Bridgeman Images.

'Send not the cat for lard.'

George Herbert, Church of England priest, c. 1600.

George's cat-calling was his way of making a particularly religious point: lead not your neighbour into temptation.

'I'm converting you all to Cat-holicism.'

A cat with a Bishop's crozier and mitre taunts mice, MS Ludwig X V 1, 15th century. From the J. Paul Getty Museum Collection.

Actus pedit pw formare i pulatus 2 Bacilo p̄
ꝰ q̄ gnotaꝰ 2 ꝓmeꝰ ꝗ̄s̄ æ dꝛoꝛ 2 aꝺ
pꝺa ꝑe ꞇelmaꝺ ꝓꝛepꞇ 2 p̄i fi̅ obeꝺieꞇꝰ ſu
ꝑe ꝛꝺꝺiꞇ ſarꝙ æ iꝛ uꞇ moꝛnar pagang̅
maꝺ fꞇa ꝛꝓꞇaꝙ ꞇꝛuꞇ eꝛgo muꝛeꝰ 2 ꝓmeꝰ
eꝛꝙ ſugꞇeꞇꝰ ꞇꝺ ꝙuo ꝑe laꞇꝛbꝛꝰ oꝛultaꞇꝰ 2
ꝓꝛueꝰ ꝯꝑtopaꞇu depopuꞇ moꝛalꝰ   ꜰoꝛe
muꝗꝛo ꝑe ꝓbbꝺꝛꝺꝺ ſſeꞇ qꝺ ab eꝛꝙ ꝺouma ꝯu ꝛdle
pluꝺ no poſꞇ ꞇuaꝛe leꝺuꝰ ꞇ̅ ꝑe ꝓꞇaꞇi alꞇꝺꝯ pub
ꞇli poꝺꝯ æ ꝺiffiꞇiliꝰ

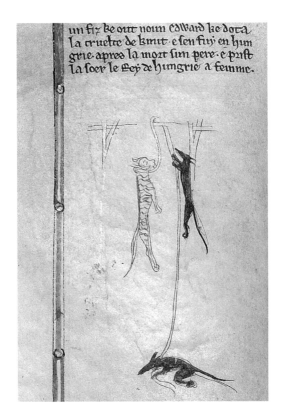

un fiz be out noun colvard ke dota
la cruelte de kmit. e sen fiuj en him
gue. apres la moxt sun pere. e puist
la soer le sex de himgrie a femme.

'Hang in there, baby!'

Two mice executing a cat, Genealogical Chronicle of the
English Kings, *England, MS Royal 14 B. V, 1275. From
the British Library archive/Bridgeman Images.*

Fain would the cat fish eat, but she is loth to wet her feet.

('The cat longs for fish, but he does not want to wet his paws.')

This famous cat proverb first appeared in 1562 but it gets a major doth of the cap in Shakespeare's *Macbeth* (1606), when in Act 1, Scene 7, Lady Macbeth calls Macbeth a coward for being unable to murder King Duncan. 'Like the poor cat i' the adage,' she says: Macbeth wants the throne but he doesn't want to get his hands dirty in order to get it.

Rubbed the Right Way

Cats hate being rubbed the wrong way, but they do love rubbing up against humans. A cat rubs its head against people's legs as a way to mark them with a scent emitted from the glands located on their head. This is a territorial marking known as *bunting*.

Cat Fact #3

60 bushels of grain

– The fine to be paid by anyone who killed an adult cat per medieval German law.

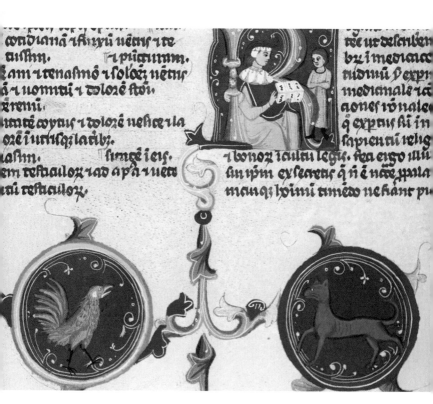

'Why did the cat cross the road? To prove he wasn't a chicken!'

A rooster and a cat square off, Claude Galien, Biblioteca Malatestiana, Italy, MS.d.xxv, c.14ᵗʰ century. From Luisa Ricciarini/Bridgeman Images.

'And where do you think
you're going?'

*Cats with runaway rats, bestiary, Royal MS 12 C XIX, f.36v, 1200.
From the British Library archive/Bridgeman Images.*

When all candles be out, all cats be gray.

('We're all the same in the dark.')

Thomas Heywood, *Book of Proverbs*, 1547.

Heywood was fond of using cats to make human points. He also famously wrote, 'A woman hath nine lives like a cat,' which is in no way biologically true.

ior sollicitudo. martirii iior xp̄
erant templi. Et eos qui i ciuita
ta sollicitudo liebant. p̄ his sctm
litia ōs spirarēt iudiciu sctm
exercitus erat ordinat. lestie e
o in leco proposita. Esidiiis maca
tru die ꝶ grauati uaqui armi
stiaꝝ. Extendēs man in cœliu
sin iuocauit. q̄ nō sctm armo
tibi place̅ꝶ dat dignis uictoꝝ
li nio. Tu dn̄e qui musisti a
ta tege tuē ꝶ i iisericordia de eas
u. d̄. Et nic dn̄ator celoꝝ mi
ii ante nos i timore ꝶ tirmo
hu tuu. ut metuāt q̄ cū blas
diiib; scm xp̄im tuū. Et his
elichanoꝝ aꝶ qui cū ip̄o erā
mouebit. ludeus tio ꝶ qui cū
p ozone ꝶ cessioie ꝶ gisti siut.
nates. Et dm̄ coroib; orante
ꝶ xp̄o. d̄. p̄sencia di magni
cessassēt ꝶ cū gaudio reduit
ꝶ rie tuisse cū armis siue. fro
dn̄ eē ciuitata pꝶa uice oi
tcebit. Precepit a iudas ꝶ p̄
ior xp̄ ciuib; pirnat eiut cap
ti cum hu iio. Abscisa ꝶ ietoso

op̄ mōstris. Et in his quoꝝ g
a principio tractido m̄ nō neg
ti ordo. nūc. disp̄o. uꝶ rō. d̄
z̄. qui fir̄z er miie tc̄r ob l
passo i carne. omnia in ci
ca in sem etiō testigis in
prib; filio ꝶ filui nom pli u
cipio sit siue ostendēs unit
ciuo eiiis glio utile z desidi
media uꝶ p̄sca ꝶ gnoscē u
uiuglu ꝶ illcarm d̄m can
sa legēre intelligit. atq; i
sisti ꝶ apii ende eiprait tra
studio ꝶ argumia siut ꝶ fid̄ f
di intellindam diligent cē c
Actis cū pmo s̄ilica
iudea. uolēe tristre a
scpsit helurate ꝶ filib; a qu
teliquid. Sic n̄. nar̄ siut ꝶ
glin s̄ilicari stei q̄ liticus e
iui scripserint ꝶ tuortiu a
p̄ ꝶ tioꝝ miidi p̄te ficē u
st est ꝶ tuortote in q̄ driga
dioru eūiglu ꝶ geis iiii
p̄ptium eoꝝ erat s̄ilice u
cū euiglia deciduit nec n
uolebit p̄ fintu niim cim

9.

NINETH LIVETH

ine lives it is said a cat possesses. Alas, 'tis not true, sadly. Nor would cats care to live more than once. To a cat, life is not about purpose, meaning or even being awake. It's about simply finding a moment and living in it for as long as possible, be it a warm lap, a furry friend or a vermin to vanquish. If this book teaches us anything about life, it's this: be more cat.

White cat jumps across a column, Arras, France, MS Codex 724, f. 272v, c.1200. From the University of Pennsylvania, Rare Book & Manuscript Library.

'Be quiet, you silly ass!'

Cat plays a tabor, a type of medieval drum, The Queen Mary Psalter, England, MS Royal 2 B. VII, f.194, 1310. From the British Library archive/Bridgeman Images.

Ways to Skin a Cat*

The cruel practice of skinning cats for pelts was all the rage in the Middle Ages, even if knights were not allowed to be caught dead in them, according to the Sumptuary Laws of 1363.** Cat skinning has now been outlawed in America and Britain – but only since 2000 and 2007, respectively.

* FYI, according to research, 24 cats are needed to make a cat fur coat for an average-sized human.

**Cat furs were considered low quality and were only allowed for 'esquires and gentlemen under the rank of knight with land worth up to £100 a year'.

Ailouros

The Ancient Greek word for 'cat' meaning 'the thing with the waving tail'.

Like the Ancient Egyptians, the Ancient Greeks loved cats. The famed historian Herodotus noted in 440 BCE that in Ancient Egypt, when a cat died, the entire family would start a deep state of grief and mourning by first shaving off their eyebrows.

'Fancy a claws encounter?'

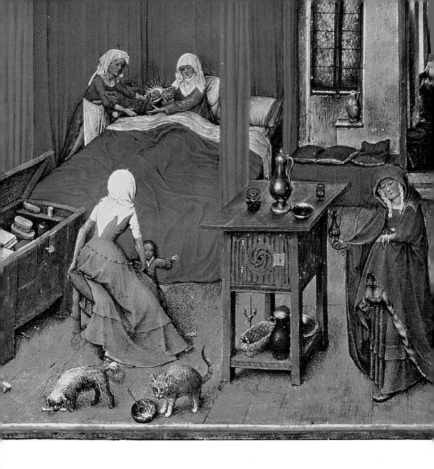

'Oh God, not another one.'

'The Birth of John the Baptist and the Baptism of Christ' + cat,
The Hours of Milan, Jan van Eyck, f.93v, 1422. Above: From
Bridgeman Images. Left: Cat coat of arms, Zürich armorial,
AG 2760, f. 1r, Schweizerisches Nationalmuseum, c. 1340.

'Nothing can stop me now!'

Ailurophile
A lover of cats.

Ailurophobia
A persistent and excessive fear of cats.

Tachotechnoailurophobia*
A terrifying fear of cats with jet packs.

* (Maybe.)

'This'll make my zoomies even zooooooomier!'

Rocket-powered cats, Ein wahres Probiertes und Pracktisches geschriebenes
Feuerbuch, *V.b.311, f. 129r, Folger Shakespeare Library, 1607. Above:
Universitätsbibliothek Heidelberg, Cod. Pal. germ. 128, f.74r, 1535.*

A black cat, I've heard it said,
Can charm all ill away,
And keep the house wherein she dwells
From fever's deadly sway.

Welsh folklore rhyme

In Celtic mythology, black cats were sacred creatures.
Scottish folklore told of how a black cat's arrival
at a new home signified prosperity and Welsh lore
stated that a black cat brought only good health.

'A mouse that has but one hole is quickly eaten!'

Cat hunts mouse into a hole, Ormesby Psalter, *MS Douce 366*,
f.131r, 1250. © *Bodleian Libraries, University of Oxford.*

'I DEMAND THE
STRING NOW!'

St Gertrude of Nivelles, portrayed as a nun, with a spindle and a cat holding wool, The Maastricht Hours (Netherlands), MS Stowe 17, f.34, 1310. From the British Library archive/Bridgeman Images.

The Wife of Bath

Thou said this, that I was like a cat;
For if anyone would singe a cat's skin,
Then would the cat well stay in his dwelling;
And if the cat's skin be sleek and gay,
She will not stay in house half a day,
But forth she will go, before any day be dawned,
To show her skin and go yowling like a cat in heat.

Geoffrey Chaucer, The Wife of Bath, The Canterbury Tales, *c.1400.*

This is one of the most famous tales from *The Canterbury Tales* and one in which a wife, Alisoun, explains to the reader that her ex-husband once compared her to a cat. It goes on a bit.

William Baldwin's 1553 *Beware the Cat* has a claim to be the first novel ever published in English. It is filled with fantastical tales of talking cats, witches disguised as grimalkins and a cat-court run by deliberating felines. It's also an anti-Catholic satire that criticises the cruel religious treatment of cats during the late medieval period. The title's ironic, then.

'Dogs and arrows?
That's overkill, guys.'

Cat stuck up a tree, The Book of The Hunt, *MS 27, f. 97, 87.MR.34.97,1430. The J. Paul Getty Museum Collection.*

'Let me out!
I'm claws-trophobic!'

Friendly cat, Aberdeen Bestiary, *MS 24, f.8v, 1200.*
From University of Aberdeen Library.

'The devyl playeth ofte with
the synnar, lyke as the catte
doth with the mous.'

('The Devil plays with our souls, like the cat plays with the mouse.')

*William Caxton (not a cat person), pioneer of the
printing press,* The Royal Book, *1484.*

'You've got something between your teeth.'

Cat Síth

The origin of the expression 'cats have nine lives' dates back to Celtic mythology, around 700 CE, and the wicked creatures known as Síth cats. The Celtics believed that these large black cats, with a stroke of white fur on their chests, were witches with the ability to transform into a cat nine times during their life. In cat form, the Síth used their sorcery to steal the souls of recently deceased humans, robbing them of the chance to ascend to Heaven. The myth of the Síth was inspired by the increasing hybridisation of wildcats and domestic cats found in Scotland during the early medieval age.

'Cats at the back,
pay attention, please.'

Jesus talks to the animals (the cats aren't listening), Aberdeen Bestiary,
MS 24, f.2v, f.5r, and f.23v, 1200. From University of Aberdeen Library.

Above: Cats, lions and a dragon, Leonardo da Vinci, c.1517. From the Royal Collection Trust/© His Majesty King Charles III, 2024/Bridgeman Images.

Opposite: A young boy with a cat, Leonardo da Vinci, F 263 inf. sheet 89 recto, 1495. Gift of Charles Rosenbloom/Bridgeman Images.

'I decide when the cuddle's over. Got it?'

'Even the smallest feline is a masterpiece of nature.'

Leonardo da Vinci, Italian painter, engineer, scientist, theorist, sculptor, architect, all-round genius, c. 1530.

Leonardo da Vinci absolutely adored cats. When he was not busy reinventing the wheel, da Vinci drew loads of sketches of kitties at play. Sadly, none of these drawings were completed as paintings.

187

erapet wreat tuius exoue lhuto nuus tuo ex
capta ta rete. et autem dux ggit.

Vsio applatur ex muutbz nteruit cet
hiit uulgue cattum a captura uo
cant. Aly dint cp capeat. 2. uidet nam tan
to actte ceruit ut fulgore lu
minum uottus tenebras supet
unde agro uenit cattus. 2. in
genosus.

Vs puellium animalg cum nomei
est: qui ceund uetu ex eo nahit lati
num fit. Alij dicunt muures cp per humore
terre nascantur. 2 nam muus
tra muus hiis in pleni luuto
uetur crescit siut quedam ma
ritima augetur. que uurtue
inunuente luna deficiunt.

alpa dicta cp sit damata cectate ppe
tua tenebus. et enim absop oculus sp
tam sodit. Hi muum egerit. 2 radices subt
terugibz commedit quod gra
alphala uocat.

nuum a nome auuum.
sz gst diuisum. nam
sit ue sibi diffunt uta nate
diuisitate. nam alie simplices sunt ut col
umbe hasiute ut pdix. alie ad mauum se
sbuuunt ut autipities. alie reformidaut

quecp du
ta do subl
lucres a
bulate d
pedie su
quarum
pulli di
quadru
uus pul
sunt uu
enibz pe
usum. u
ac tou ea
uolanie
penna
dut et pl
quadru
uus non
opsita u
ulula cu
tas enui
Tul
tta
cipitet uo
Z ultra n
caunt. Al
tes. mult
scuritate

10.

THE CATT OUTTETH THE BAGGETH

anding on their feet at the end of the medieval era, cats were quick to lord their torturous treatment all over us. Never again would they find themselves stuffed in a sack, drowned in a river, burnt to a crisp or skinned alive by sorcerors. The cats were once again out the bag, back in charge, and living life large...

Cats love a good box, Dares Phrygius, History of the Trojan War III, *Alexander Neckam, De nuptiis Philologiae et Mercurii fabula IV, R.14.9, f.100r, England, 12th century. From the Master and Fellows of Trinity College and Trinity College Wren Library, Cambridge.*

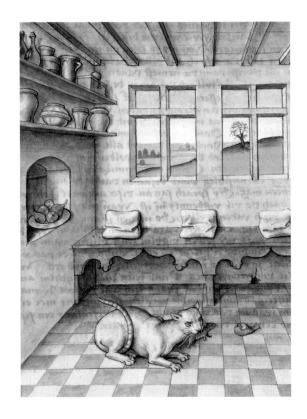

'Any mousehole's a goal!'

A cat catches a mouse outside a hole, Fables of Bidpai,
MS 680/1389, f.96, Wurtenburg, Germany, c.1480. ©
Musée Condé, Chantilly/Bridgeman Images.

Medieval Dates for Your Diary

525 – The invention of
the Anno Domini calendar

717 – The Siege of Constantinople, the most
important military conflict of the Middle Ages

800 – Charlemagne crowned emperor of the Romans

919 – First use of gunpowder

1066 – The Battle of Hastings, and the
Norman conquest of England

1095 – The Crusades begin (and go on for ages)

1215 – *The Magna Carta*, the beginning of
the end for the powerful monarchs

1347 – The Black Death, the largest pandemic
in human history; 200 million dead

1439 – Johannes Gutenberg invents the printing press

1492 – Italian explorer Christopher
Columbus sets sail to the Americas

The medieval era, or Middle Ages, is
subdivided into three distinct periods:

Early – sometimes referred to as
the Dark Ages, from 475

High – from 1000

Late – from 1300

'Snug as a cat in a hat.'

Cat snail, Book of Hours (*Netherlands*), Stowe 17, *f.185, 1310.*
From the British Library archive/Bridgeman Images.

'Have a good poke around,
why don't you.'

Cat stabbin', bestiary, MS. e Mus. 136, c.1275. ©
Bodleian Libraries, University of Oxford.

'They delight in being stroked by the hand of a person and they express their joy with their own form of singing.'

Thomas de Cantimpré, on why cats purr, De natura rerum (On the Nature of Things), *1270.*

'Game over, rodent!'

'Take the gull of a male cat, and the fat of a hen all white, and mix them together, and anoint thy eyes, and thou shalt see it that others cannot see.'

Albertus Magnus's recipe for a 'magical' cat potion, The Book of Secrets, c.1245. Albertus had many other 'remedies' that involved cats, including rubbing a cat's tail in your eye to cure a stye. It doesn't work. We tried.

'Eight lives left.'

Startled cat chased up a tree by a pack of dogs, MS Ludwig XV 1, f.44, 83.MR.171.44, France, 1500. From The J. Paul Getty Museum Collection.

omo volens in navicula brachium mare[s]
deu[m] rogab[at] ut ei assisteret et ad opta[...]
[...]ret media a via s[an]c[t]a irruit in navicula[m] [...]
assere cepit et ille t[..]dare Rogauit ergo [...]
unde exiuit cu[m] i[n]mittet p[ro] eu[m] i[p]se i[n]m[...]
obuiantib[us] undis et i[m]pedit[...] [...]ue ergo des[...]
t[...] citius venire poss[et] ait ad d[omi]n[u]m fac m[...]
tate tua et quo facere mea [...] vis et sto[...]
i[m]pul[sus] flatib[us] optato lit[...] e[st] [...]atut[...] [...]
[...]m voluntate[m] sua[m] divin[e] subi[ect]a voluntati [...]
[...]m in periculis a deo n[on] delinqu[...]

Cat Fact #4

America's 'first' pet cat breed – the American Shorthair – are all descended from the cats that travelled on *The Mayflower* with the British colonists in 1620. The cats aboard the ship, en route to Cape Cod, were employed to keep rats and mice away from food rations. Once the ship arrived, the cats were free to live in the land of liberty and be witnesses to the birth of the nation.

'Two for the price of one!'

*Cat chasing mouse (with a mouse on its back), bestiary
(Rochester), England, Royal 12 F.XIII, f.43r, c.1250. From
the British Library archive/Bridgeman Images.*

Cats versus Dogs

The phrase 'Fighting like cats and dogs' dates back to at least 1611, but is likely much more medieval in origin. Shakespeare (him again!) certainly knew of their disdain for each other. In his tragedy, *Hamlet* (1603), the titular hero mutters, 'The cat will mew and the dog will have its day,' (Act 5, Scene 1).

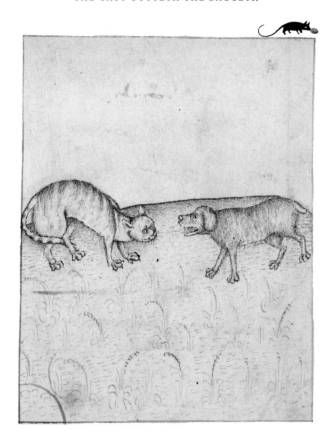

'Your dog days are over, mate.'

'To Agree Like Cat and Dog', *Léon Gruel, Savoy, France,*
W.313.30R, 1490. From the Walters Art Museum, Baltimore.

201

lectationes 11

a usq; in fine

or

fa

&

luntatem tu

aun . ut clar

Nepeta cataria

The Latin name for catnip, a perennial herb in the mint family. Catnip contains a chemical called nepetalactone that hilariously affects a cat's behaviour when ingested or rubbed into fur. When high, cats enjoy a 15-minute period of intense zaniness and drooling followed by equally intense sleeepiness.

'Here come the tickle paws!'

A cat playing with its kitten, Psalter, MS Ashmole 1525, f.014r, c.13th century. © Bodleian Libraries, University of Oxford.

'Whenever thou sits to eat at the table, avoid the cat on the bare wood, for if thou strokes a cat or a dog, thou art like an ape tied with a lump of wood.'

James Orchard Halliwell, The Boke of Curtasye
(The Book of Courtesy), *1475.*

By the 15th century, cats lived indoors with their owners. But allowing the cat near the dining table while humans ate was still regarded as the height of bad manners, according to medieval codes of social etiquette.

'Your breath smells
worse than mine – and I've
been licking my butt!'

Cat kissing, Book of Hours (Rome), MS B. 11. 22, f.38r,
*c.1440. From the Master and Fellows of Trinity College
and Trinity College Wren Library, Cambridge.*

'I don't need the devil
to possess a human –
I can do that all by myself.'

Evil cat, bestiary, CCA-LitMs/D/10 fol. 11r, c.1300. ©
Canterbury Cathedral/Reproduced courtesy of the
Chapter, Canterbury Cathedral/Bridgeman Images.

'Dryve out dogge and catte, or els geve them a clout.'

John Russell, The Boke of Nature, *1460.*

◇◇

It is clear from John Russell's well-read publication, *The Boke of Nature*, that as the medieval era ended pets were still not allowed to sleep – or even enter – the bedroom of their owners. Perhaps Russell's quote is the origin of the idiom 'kick the cat'?

'Catch you later!'

Three lions on a church, Salisbury Cathedral, Wiltshire, England. This famous cathedral was built in 1220 and houses one of only four surviving copies of the Magna Carta, *one of the most important documents created in the medieval era, c.1215.*

208